CAN
YOU
IMAGINE?

Human being now live in a world full of illusion,
where people are greatly misled, values are
thrown away and impiety are embraced

JOHNSON BENJAMIN

PARTRIDGE
A Penguin Random House Company

ISBN: Hardcover   978-1-4828-9612-1
          Softcover   978-1-4828-9611-4
          eBook   978-1-4828-9281-9

To order additional copies of this book, contact
Toll Free 800 101 2657 (Singapore)
Toll Free 1 800 81 7340 (Malaysia)
orders.singapore@partridgepublishing.com

www.partridgepublishing.com/singapore

DEDICATION

To God my all in all
And to great and inspiring minds who truly love and cares for
others, even if it makes them different.

ACKNOWLEDGMENT

*E*ver praise and thanks to the Almighty God, the creator of all things.

Of necessity, my lovely wife, my daughter, my parents and siblings deserve big thanks for their love and ceaseless prayers offered to God for my success. May the good Lord continue to keep and bless you all.

Special mention must be made of the Rev. N. T. Akambe who took time to write a "foreword" to this book. I also applaud Pastor E.A. Andrew who continually encouraged me to publish this volume. Do accept my tremendous gratitude.

I am grateful to Norlin Binte Ngasewan (Singapore) and my dear friends who have inspired me through their jokes, quotes, true life stories and many more who stirred me through their deed and response. I am greatly pleased.

Finally, a big thanks to you for reading this book for without you this book will not be written.

I am delighted to be encouraged by you all.

FOREWORD

The volume in your hand is a motivational thriller. Every line of every page has motivational, encouraging and inspiring energy that would not be got anywhere else except by reading this book. Written in the most colorful and thought provoking language, every thought is supported by a true life story of personal experience or that of a close acquaintance the end product being an exceptional book presented to you in living colors.

The bottom-line is that no one, you too, reads this book from cover to cover and remains the same because it has an automotive power to cause spontaneous change in one's disposition and position in intention and by extension; it is a deliberate design of the author, his gift to you. Rushing to finish this book or keeping it aside without acting on it is a double tragedy. Take your time, read it digestively to understand and apply its values in daily life and smile to a transformed life.

This book is written with you in mind; for you and your entire family invest in it, grab copies for your family now and you will never regret you did. It is the best investment, gift and inheritance you will give to your children and friends. At the end of the book you will not remain the same.

It's a promise!

Nenge, Terna Akambe

INTRODUCTION

*W*hether you just bought this book or it somehow landed before you, it's an opportunity because this volume is crammed with issues that challenge our modern day thinking. How we as human have constantly embrace war instead of peace and hatred instead of love. As you read along you will be required to do some experiment using your mind's eye and logical thinking to judge your action and reaction on day-to-day basis. If you can imagine, you may be asked to suspend your belief, then think about those issues that make you feel strange or irrational, think about those tradition that you observe, those judgments that you quickly pass without even knowing the root of the matter, those things you were compelled to do which are now part of you and then have a rethink.

Written in simple terms such that it would be easy to read and understand. You can flip it open anytime to any page and get something of great value from it. Although it is written in nugget and illustrations, its content will cause you to look at the paradox of our time and the world around you in ways that will make you think differently. The pages are invaluably filled with valuable illustration that does not only excite you, but makes you to think of the absurdity of our age.

Think of it, our generation as an increasingly visual-oriented one has a history of advance science and technology where we see skyscrapers, wider freeways, but narrower viewpoints and massive accidents. A survey reveals that a great number of people spend more than they earn to impress people they don't even love, they buy more, but enjoy less and die miserably.

We are in a world where judgments are passed easily without even knowing the root of the case or real investigation, where those who steal billion are sentenced to just three months in prison or even discharged and acquitted and thereafter reappointing them as ministers, while those who steals food to feed their hungry belly are sentenced to 15 years in prison or even killed. This is a world where the judicial system uses adjournment as winning tools to free culprits of their choice.

Where the rich build bigger houses with ill gotten money, but they have small families to live there, they want to be more convenient even though they have less time to live. People acquire more degrees, but are becoming less human with less sense; in fact they have more knowledge, but when it comes to building and executing projects to eradicate poverty, they perform abysmally. No wonder we have more experts, yet expert ignorance is ubiquitous.

In this generation there are more pharmacies manufacturing different kinds of medicine, yet more people are yet people are dying of different disease. We are faced with more teachers and professors, yet we have educated illiterates and half baked graduates. This generation drink much more than the past generations put together, smoke much more, spend thoughtlessly, laugh too little, drive too fast, they get extreme too easily and do not care to suicide, they throw explosives and bombs in the churches and market places. They stay up too late to club, get up too tired, read too little, watch TV too much, and pray too seldom.

No doubt, with the help of information and telecommunication technology (ICT) this generation have multiplied its possessions, but has constantly reduced its values. We have manufactured different weapon of mass destruction, warships, drones, but little of world peace, love and brotherliness. We talk too much on things that should be done, but do very little, we love through clenched teeth. In fact racism is still on the increase and people still hate others without course. Nations easily fight with one another rather than embracing one another. People easily learned how to make a living, but not a life. We've added years to life, not life to years. No doubt it is stated that in our generation "We have killed more than we have helped to live. We've been all the way to the moon and back, but have trouble crossing the street to meet the new neighbor. We've conquered outer space, but not inner space. We've done larger things, but not better things. We've cleaned up the air, but polluted the soul. We've split the atom, but not our prejudice. We write more, but learn less."

Now just think of this. We are in a world where African presidents promises more, plan more, but accomplish nothing or very little, they just hang on in spite of their ineptitude and unfaithfulness to the oath of office. They prefer to die in office to stepping aside for a young pragmatic and prolific leader. CAN YOU IMAGINE? "We've learned to rush, but not to wait. We build more computers to hold more information, to produce more copies than ever, but we communicate less and less. These are the times of fast foods and slow digestion; big men, and small character; where a home minister of a country will tell the citizen to leave the country if they are unhappy. These are days of two incomes, but more divorce; fenced houses, but broken homes.

These are days of quick trips, disposable diapers, throwaway morality, one night stands, overweight bodies, and pills that do everything from cheer, to quiet, to kill. It is a time when there is much in the show window and nothing in the stockroom."

As this book unveils these ills, think about how you can make the world a better place in your own little way.

What would the world say of you when you are long gone? Are you here to destroy or you are here to love and to build. Now stop for a minute and just imagine. What have you been building? Well, Orison Swett Marden was right when he said "the universe is one great kindergarten for men. Everything that exists has brought with it its own peculiar lesson".

Above all, the quintessence of this book is not to add new information or belief as it is to add to your mind or try to convince you of anything, but to bring about a shift in your imagination and sense of reasoning to identify, analyze, and stand out for the right to build a stronger and better generation.

It's about you . . . yes you.

I am certain that at some point in each person's life there comes a time when he or she crave for growth and expression on one thing or the other. It could be when you struggle to overcome limitation or when you move violently to achieve increase in who you want to be. As a result of this, a great number of people become conscious that it is not just birth, growth, good health, achievement, enjoyment, and victory, but also disappointment, breakdown, bad health, bereavement, putrefy, ache, and lost. As you grow, you begin to learn what is good and what is bad. Having grown to a certain stage you no longer need much preaching to differentiate what is "good" and what is "bad". Hence you begin to know yourself and you think that nobody can tell you who you are better than you. And if they do, it would just be another concept, so it would not change you. You are who you truly belief you are no doubt. However, the true "you" is God's desire for you and until you know this, you will be like a poor tramp that is not acquainted with the fact that he has a billion dollars in the bank and so his wealth remains dormant.

As you think of who you are, think also of who you are not because this book will be reflecting on what you think and what you do to your generation. Remember, thinking isolates a situation and call it "can" or "cannot" therefore, if you think you can make a change, you are right and if you think you cannot, you are also right. In other words, what you think you are and what you perceive determines your sense of who you are, and what you do in life. What is it that gets you upset and makes you want to act irrational, is it driven by religion, culture, tradition, or race? Examine yourself again to find out how truly you know yourself, because whatever matters to you may have the influence to sadden you to do things that are not expected of you. It is not necessarily what you speak or accept as true that matters, but what your action and reactions reveals are as important and as serious to you and others. Consequently you may want to ask yourself a question, what are the things that upset and hurt people? If love, peace, joy, happiness, unity, and progress matters to you than anything else, and if you truly know yourself to be a great human rather than a little you, you will remain nonreactive and absolute alert when confronted with challenging thoughts, people or situations.

**Even if I know that tomorrow the world will go to
pieces, I would still plant my apple tree**

—Martin Luther

While I was growing up I really like listening to news, back home it's usually at 9:00pm. Many times I just sit for a long time listening to people and government as they talk about what should be done, plans to take for a better country. If you really observe with me today you will notice that more has been done to satisfy self than the country they took oath to serve. In fact we now live in the time when it is frightening to be alive, when it is hard to think of human being as rational creature. Everywhere we look we see brutality, stupidity, war and racism. Recently if you watch the news, it seems that there is nothing else to be seen but indecent manner, war, bombing, weapons of mass destruction and barbarism. Everywhere you tune to; you see corruptions which are unable to check. I am sure that while it is true that there is a general worsening situation, it is precisely because things are so frightening we become hypnotized, and do not notice, or if we do notice, we refused to fight it strongly.

We live in a time were people are living with extreme fear and tension. Not just where I came from, but all over the world. Many countries are now at alert; they spend money they ought to use for human welfare to build weapons, to waging war and to intercept missiles. Having analyzed the global circumstances Albert Einstein said, "The world is a dangerous place to live; not because of the people who are evil, but because of people who don't do anything about it.

I have a premonition that someday and very soon this insanity must be searched for by precisely judging our own behavior and returning to God who thought us to love one another. Imagine a country where people who stole and emblaze public funds in the name of service, killing people and subjecting many children fatherless, are at liberty, but sentencing and executing people who merely stole chicken, because they have no food to eat. What

5

will become of our generation in the nearest future, when people look back at our time, will they be happy how great a people we are, or will they be amazed at our stupidity know how strong and developed we were but have constantly failed because of our stupidity. Personally, what would people say of you when you are long gone? What and how would you want to be remembered?

I see some people's beauty. Not in their dressing, not in their wealth, not even the way they speak, just who they are.

A few times I spend a good deal of time in the toilet wondering how human being will seem to their maker when simple instructions are thrown away. I mean giving thanks in every situation; of course it may be argued that this is a fairly bleak view of life. One may ask, "does it mean that I should thank God even when am wrongly persecuted?" well it may seem difficult because you think it's an extraordinary thing to do, but there is a blessing in a thankful heart.

Just few days ago I read the story of a seventy years old man who was affected by a disease which made him unable to urinate. The doctors told him that he needs an operation to cure the disease . . . He agreed to do the operation as the problem was giving him severe pain for days. When the operation was completed the doctor gave him a bill which covered all the costs. After looking at the bill, the man started crying upon seeing this, the doctor said "Sir, you don't have to cry, if the cost is too high then we could make some other arrangements for you." The old man replied, "I am not crying because of the money, but I am crying because God loves me, He freely made me urinate for seventy years and He never sent me a bill!" often times you just walk freely, you do anything you want to do and you always forget to say "thank you Lord" think of your ability to move, to eat, to see, to talk, to read, to sleep, to think and so on. Have you thanked God for His countless blessings today?

Sometime you just want to do it your way, but just think for a minute. Can you really do anything without God's help? In a wedding reception the MC just gave a joke that made me think all through. He said "there was an interview with God "The man asked: "dear God, what surprises you most about man?" God smile and replied "That man got bored with childhood; they rush to grow up, and long to be children again. They lose their health to make money and then lose their money to restore health. That they think anxiously about the future and they forget the present, such that they live neither in the present nor the future. He said that man live as if they will never die and die as though they never lived.

The world is my country,
all mankind are my brethren,
and to do good is my religion.

—Thomas Paine

Generally, by now one would think that people are conscious of the differences between tradition, spirituality and religion, far from it. A misunderstanding of these three rudiments can ruin your life. While Tradition is simply the passing down of elements of culture from one generation to another, people confuse Spirituality with Religion, it's not. Though it may be affiliated with religion, but in quintessence it is searching to know your real self and to discover the true nature of consciousness. Religion even though it is difficult to defined, I gleaned that it is an organized collection of beliefs, cultural systems and world views that relates humanity to the supernatural, and to spirituality. Having a believe system or a set of idea that you regard as absolute truth does not make you spiritual. In fact, Many "Religious" people are confused, they contradict their beliefs by equating the truth with their thought or ideas and they claim to be in lone custody of the truth. They fail to realize the limitation of their thought. If you don't believe or think the way they do, you are wrong in their eyes and they feel justified in killing you for that. What a people!!! Although some religion institution will be open to the new understanding whether good or bad; others continue to harden their doctrinal positions and become part of those manmade structures. While many are neither cold not hot, a few hold firm to the truth.

Today, extremisms and alteration of consciousness, is rising to a large extent outside of the formation of the existing institutionalized religions. Just recently a sudden monolithic trend is spring up; the west is trying to enforce their latest belief on the entire world by introducing same sex marriage. **Can you imagine?** The same people who translated and preached the Bible are now contradicting it. We are witnessing not only an unprecedented influx of our time. Look at this teenager, Malala

Yousafzai, she is a Pakistan girl who narrowly escaped death by gunshot from the Taliban's group, because she is promoting education for all. As she addresses the world leaders on her sixteenth birthday, she said something about the man who shot her. She said "Even if there is a gone in my hand and he stands in front of me, I will not kill him". What a kind speech! She was trained to forgive, to love and to make peace not to kill because one is of different belief. If you are unable to look beyond forms and religion, then you may be going extremely badly.

We are, perhaps, uniquely among the earth's creatures, the worrying animal. We worry away our lives, fearing the future, discontent with the present, unable to take in the idea of dying, unable to sit still

—Lewis Thomas

Sometime we find ourselves at a strangely familiar juncture looking both backward and forward simultaneously not knowing what to do or say. Well, this scenario happened in late 1990's. A boy and his dad went to a city's main market somewhere in West Africa for shopping and suddenly, a young man ran past them carrying a bundle of lace materials. While they stood raining obscenities at him for pushing people roughly, a trader ran out of her shop shouting "**Ole! Ole!! Ole!!!** (thief! Thief!! Thief!!!) Immediately they knew she was referring to the guy who just ran past them. The boy's dad being a strict disciplinarian followed in hot pursuit alongside many others. They hadn't gone far when they saw a mob gathered around a young man, beating him with sticks and chains.

The boy's dad tried to push forward to tell them that they were beating the wrong man, but the stares he was given were enough to say "back away old man, or you join him". Something was terribly wrong they thought; this wasn't the man who ran out of the store with those clothes. They were happy to see the Yoruba trader screaming at the top of her voice. "**No be am, no be am tif my cloth**". (He is not the one who stole my clothes) but the noise of the blood thirsty citizens drowned out her voice as they watched a man bring a tire and throw around this young man's neck.

Then the boy looked up, and spotted the man who ran with those items in the crowd. Watching and waiting. Their eyes met and he nudged at his dad with fear and when his dad looked in the direction of his face and saw him too. This time, the man was disappearing into the crowd. As this was happening I could feel the young man as he was burning shouting at the top of his voice, with his last strength (*Am innocent! Lord help me!! Why me lord!!!*) In our generation we find it easy to pass judgments, life no longer means a thing to some people. Ask yourself, have you in anyway murdered anyone either physically or through your gossip. Now think of it. This story doesn't mean that all victims of rabble actions are not guilty, what it means is when the primitive urge in man, frustrations and lack of trust in our legal stems push us to the edge, we should always watch and be careful because something may perhaps go terribly wrong.

I gathered that God doesn't propose to judge a man
until he is dead, so why should you?

Humans most times are unpredictable, it is a fact that faces all of us especially when we try to figure out what others do and we fail to comprehend them. Behavior that seems to have no meaning or purpose will always keep people off-balance, and they will wear themselves out trying to understand. Some days ago I was having lunch with two of my course mates in the cafeteria of the graduate school at the University of East London where I was studying.

Something happened and it reminded me about the story of a 50 years old man who was sitting with his 25years old son in the train. The train was about to leave the station, all passengers were settling down on their seats. As the train gradually moves the young man was filled with lots of joy and curiosity. He was sitting on the window side where he could see and observe the nature clearly without any obstruction. He stretched out one of his hand outside the window as he feels the air. He shouted, "Papa see all the trees are going behind" the old man smiled and admire his feelings. Beside the young man was a couple sitting and listening to all the conversation between the father and son. They were little awkward with the attitude of the 25 years old son behaving like a small child.

Suddenly the young man again shouted "papa see!!! The pond and animals, again he shouted, papa! The cloud is moving with train". The couples were watching the young man embarrassingly. Now it was raining again and some of the waters dropped touching the young man's hand. He felt with joy and closed his eyes. He shouted again, "Papa it is raining, water is touching me, see papa see, papa see". The couple couldn't help themselves, but asked the old man. "Why don't you visit the doctor and get some treatment for your son". The old man replied and said,

"Yes we are coming from the hospital, we are so happy because today, my son got his eyes sight for the first time in his life. Have you been so fast in judging other people because you have the opportunity and freedom? Wait a minute and think again. Do not judge until you know all the facts.

There's a great power in words, if you don't hitch too many of them together

—Josh Billing

While flying back from Singapore with a Jet Airline on 19th January 2013 I pulled out a book from the back seat just before me to relax my mind while we fly. I noticed that it was a piece of work written by someone who seeks to address the ill spoken words of our time. He viewed the way people talk, without thinking and how our words could build and destroy people. He said,

"Most time in life we tend to say things that either make or mar a relationship or even cause harm. Speaking comes naturally to most people as breathing. On most occasions our words are uttered without any conscious thought and without weighing the consequences. Most time we hardly stop and ponder about what we are saying."

Having considered the power of observation, originality of imagination, virility of ideas and remarkable talent for narration which characterize the creations of the world-famous authors, Rudyard Kipling a Bombay born author won the Nobel award prize in 1907. He said, *"Words are, of course, the most powerful drug used by mankind."* It is a habit that most people are guilty of and are trying very hard to put a stop to, but it just keeps propping up in everything we do. But then we must realize that our words could make or mar us. As you freely speak, watch your judgment and thoughts on daily basics because words can have negative effects on you and those around you. There is great power in the word we utters, but sometime we do not realize them put them in perfect use. It is said that words are so powerful that when repeated with emotion tend to bring out some other side of us. Our words have tremendous power and could create an action in others either negatively or positively. You must think before you speak.

Having gone through this as the aircraft pierce through the air gaining balance I was just imagining and I trying to bring to mind what I said in the past few hours. Then I concluded that everything we say produces an effect in the long run. There are times when you say things out of annoyance to someone or even your spouse and they end up having a negative effect on them, some even rain obscenity on their children when they are angry. This can make them lose balance and focus which is not good for you or for them, because whatever you say to someone produces some kind of effect in that person. Therefore, think before you talk, and don't just talk, but speak.

The information you know determine how far you can go!!! If you judge people, you have no time to love them.

—Mother Teresa

Unless you are severally careful, you may be saying words that could encourage or discourage people. As I said in the previous page, we all know how powerful our words and actions are in influencing others. Your words can bring hope to others and also to yourselves, it a kind of back-up, support or depression depending how they are used. If words are used in a responsible manner it brings comfort to others and even to you especially when you are experiencing complicated situations. When you speak with caution it has an extensive lasting consequence to the person it is been spoken to, even after you are long gone, after you must have expressed them it will chime either a destructive or a helpful bell for many years to come. Therefore, you must be careful of what you say. Make your words short, simple and lovable anytime you speak because you may eat a part someday.

Flinging words without realizing the impact might be detrimental to your image and others. Once spoken, words are like bullet released from a gun and can never be stopped until it reaches its target. But the consequences can be stopped by trying to weigh your words before you utter them. Many people have memories of words that have been said to them by others and it continues to ring bell anytime they see or remember such people later in life. Some of these words were uttered without understanding how much effect it has on the recipient. A friend told us about the most important words, he said "The six most important words are: (I admit I made a mistake), the five most important words: (You did a good job), the four most important words: (What is your opinion?) The three most important words: (If you please), the two most important words: (Thank you) and the one least important word: (I.)"

Words will always remain one weapon used for the sake of peace and distribution while we all know how powerful our actions are in influencing others. You must not lose sight of how powerful your words could be. As a result of this, next time you want to say any word, pause and think before you speak because it could be destructive at the end.

Rather than focusing on what you don't have or what's out of reach, be thankful for the wonderful things already in your life and use them.

A large part of life centers on anticipation. How much we want to have in our bank account, how large we want our conglomerate to be, how long we want to live, how much we would lose if we were to wake up one day to the unexpected predicament.

Orison Swett Marden's quote is still remembered today when he said "There is no medicine like hope, no incentive so great, and no tonic so powerful as expectation of something tomorrow." Expectations! We all have them. We expect that people should be nice to us, we expect that we will have good health, we expect great marriages, we expect faithful friends, successful careers, but what do we do when life doesn't live up to our expectation?

I have come across people with broken expectation of places they expected to live or settle down, but they found themselves in different places and their expectation was shattered. I have met people in relationships and broken expectation of the future, some people realized that the relationship they are now having wasn't what they actually expected, yet they remain surprisingly upbeat. Some people even find their self in prison which is not a place of their expectation, some get stuck in a very tough marriage, some in an unrewarding job or a challenging neighborhood, which is easy to get discouragement, but above all, there is the need to be positive in whatever situation you find yourselves.

When viewed microscopically, it seems the fight is not against you; rather it is for you to prepare yourself for a great future. Many immigrants fall in this kind of circumstances, they were true believers, well trained and cultured set of people in their different home country, but because they are not spiritually matured, they now, follow the wind. They now spend their adult lives being loyal to men rather than God; they indulge in a lot of unlawful things just to make money. In fact, they make them believe that there is no God. I love Albert Camus beautiful expression about God. He said "I would rather live my life as if there is a God and die to find out there isn't, than live my life as if there isn't and die to find out there is". Don't be deceived, God knows you. Unless you change and be the person God wants you to be, the end may be regrettable.

Sometimes we all need to realize that negative thoughts have no power, we empower them.

—Kurt Goad

Believe with me, one restrained strategy of the enemy is to make you comfortable in the wilderness. He desires that you become a little more relaxed in discomforting situation instead of pushing forward for change. How do I mean? You are destined to be a great man or a great woman, but you just achieve a little in life and you think that is all you needed, and you begin to stay around your comfort zone until you lose everything that you have earned. All that the enemy wants is for you to learn to live with ill health instead of pushing for healing. The enemy wants you to accept negative status quo in your business, in your carrier and even in your study instead of pushing forward for a drastic change. According to Zig Ziglar in his book (Breaking Through the Next Level) he said "In virtually every case, you are what you are and where you are because of the choices which you have made or which have been made for you" therefore if you don't like what you are seeing, then change what you are seeing by changing what you are doing.

Hear this, don't relax, don't even accept any negative experience, continue to push for change. Isn't it amazing that people often live lives that constantly negate the basic principle of excellence by doing things so incongruous, yet they expect extraordinary people and things to come to them perfectly? Some people are kings but they seek the wise men of this world neglecting the kingship in them. While admonishing us my father will always say "Who you are will determine what you will attract. Who you are will define what will come to you. Who you are before men will determine how they treat you". So, live your life so well so that you can attract good things and the right people. As soon as you make mistakes, try again and again until you get it right. Never stay down where you have fallen, always stand and try to move on. This saying is funny, but there is a lot to learn from it. "An old man said eraser are made for those who make mistakes, but a young man replied eraser are made for those who are will to correct their mistakes." one thing is to identify your mistake and know where you have fallen, another is to correct it and move on.

**You can't give character to another person,
but you can encourage him to develop his own
by possessing one yourself**

—Artemus Calloway

Having trained them to do so, the two school children who were going back to the hostel were given instruction by their parents to always read the Bible at least twice daily. As they pack their baggage for school, their parents bought everything they needed and gave each of them a Bible as they were leaving, they prayed with them and reminded them again to read the Bible at least twice daily.

The children promised to read the Bible daily. However, inside each of the Bible was hidden seven hundred dollars without the consent of the children. The children went to school and never even opened their Bible; they were very comfortable as their parent had given them everything they needed for school. Soon after, they began to run out of cash and eventually they had no money left with them. They called home and their parents were very excited to hear from them, but after the pleasantries they complained about hardship and demanded for more money.

Their parent asked them if they have been reading the Bible, they replied yes, but they lied. Their parents knowing that they had lied ask them to go and read their Bible for two days that God will provide money for them. They dropped the phone and the son was very angry, but the daughter quietly went and picked her Bible, as she opened it, she saw the seven hundred dollars and she was so excited. She called her brother and told him what she had seen, although her brother never believed her even though he ask for some money, he still did not read his Bible. All along their parents were trying to introduce the children to read the Bible on their own, but they couldn't understand the pranks played by their parent. Oftentimes you are just within your success until the success is out of reach then you tend to look for it somewhere else, leaving the precious gifts God has given us. Now look around you, have you left something undone? Or are their things you are supposed to be doing and you left them undone because you are in abundance now. My mother will always tell us this. "If praising God is the source of your blessing then keep praising Him, if doing good is the source of our blessing then never leave it."

**Recognize your mistake and learn from them,
But don't dwell on them.**

—Zig Ziglar

Think of it, isn't it true that in life, people often go back to the things they left behind or the things they promise not to do. They often return to the unfruitful places they have left behind in the past. People often go back to unfruitful relationship; they often go back to addiction and associations. Sometimes because they are yet to experience the real change they desire, they hurriedly return to the status quo. Please don't go back to that unfruitful habit, don't go back to listen to people whose words or action adds no value to your life. To go back is to die.

Friend think of it, sometimes you fill your mind with memories of lost opportunities; you are occupied with failed dreams, you often think about failed relationships, disappointments, heartbreaks, deprivation and even how to be successful in the work you do, you worry about so many things. And you fail to take fresh steps that will take you into abundance. Don't stay in the same level that has brought you nothing. Don't limit yourself to sad experiences of the past. Take another shot at life, aim higher, go for fresh opportunities, and take new steps that will give you new results, go for fruitful relationships, attend fruitful meetings and conferences and engage yourself in discussions that add value to your life, decree and seek abundance and work towards it.

Am pragmatic about this, great achievement sometimes comes with great risk, new level comes with risk and battle, new height are loaded with circumstances we need to conquer as such you must be aggressive sometimes to get to the next level. Most times you need to take risk, yea, some may ask, what if it fails . . . Wait a minute, why can you ask another uplifting question like, "what if it succeeds?" That ostensible danger involved in the project might just be your spring board to distention. That adventure will add to your venture

I gathered that people who do nothing and risk nothing, at the end they have nothing, and they become nothing. He may avoid suffering and sorrow. However, choose to take spirit inspired risk that will usher you into greatness. Remember, you need to be part of something great.

People place the tentacles of worry and fear around the problem so that it cannot go away while some still hug their problem to their bosoms and call it "my problem".

The product of worry is fear; its resultant effect might be known or unknown to the person in question. Fear may come as a result of past experience of an individual or by the experience of other individuals which usually has a psychological effect on the individual. Fear can come as result of low self esteem, when you feel that you may be mocked or laughed at when you do what you do or intend to do and the result is wrong. Generally, people have fear of the past, present and future. Fear mostly is termed as a negative trait in some individuals. However, not all fear are for negative reasons, fear can also be for positive reasons that is to say that fear is termed into two aspects namely: Positive fear and Negative fear.

Positive fear is felt out of respect for others or a higher authority, such fear brings about peace of mind since the resultant effect is known, which can bring sadness or enmity if that fear out of respect for others or a higher authority is breached upon. Negative fear as discussed earlier can also be termed as the fear of unknown, it usually fills the mind with anxieties, worries, insecurity, depression and so many effects which leaves one in unstable state of mind, some of these can lead a person(s) to take drastic measures. Think of it, whether you worry about it or not, whatever will happen will happen. A young man went for HIV test but didn't wait for the result to be out, so he decided to take his life because he thought that he would be diagnose HIV positive, but the result was negative. A young girl left school due to the fear that she had failed the previous exams she wrote. Negative fear in a man yields negative results but positive fear such as the fear of God will always yield positive results and this is achieved by obeying His words and keeping his commandments. The fear of God is the beginning of wisdom. Charles Schulz said "Don't worry about the world coming to an end today. It is already tomorrow in Australia".

Most people see a shadow and think it is a substance. They live in fear of the unknown, dwelling in fear of things that may never happen. People sense danger and think that they are the victim already. They see economic turmoil and begin to fear the worst. They see the shadow of death and mistake it for death itself. Hear this, any danger or pain you see around you is just a shadow. Shadow may stir up fear, but cannot kill. Therefore be strong and if you must fear, fear the lord.

Time is not the problem, time is the usher
that enables us to measure our effectiveness,
how for the time we have been here,
how much have we changed

—anonymous

Tick—tack—tick—tack was the sound of the wall clock, the time was 9:55am on a Monday morning, although some students were still seen rushing to school, Mano was still on his bed sleeping. Some minutes later, he was awakened by the sound of a vehicle horn and reluctantly he rolled off the bed with a squeezed face forcing his eyes to open as the early morning sun had set. Standing in front of the door, he stretched his hands above his head for a little exercise. He walked out of the door and reluctantly sat on a wooden bench at the balcony, not mindful of the time as a student who should be in the classroom at 10am. Yet, time never waits for no one. Time happens to be one of God's gifts that is freely and evenly distributed to humankind. No human being has more time than the other; everyone has the same twenty four hours in a day, but more significantly, the usage of time differs from one person to another.

In other words, the quality of your product depends largely on the time you invested in the product. For example, if you are learning a keyboard, you must give adequate time to practice. For Mano's case, he did not value his time, his frequent absent eventually gave him a bad result. You must make good use of your time. Always ask yourself this question. **WHAT MUST I DO TODAY TO REALLY USE MY TIME?** At the end of the day you must evaluate how you have used your time. Is it really worth it? Time, how powerful it is even though many people disvalue it. It is so unfortunate that 55% of this generation lose a whole lot because of perpetual abuse of time. Time abuse could mean excessive use of time or using time unfairly. Time is so precious, it is only time that differentiate events, it is only time that helps us to differentiates activities and or events not to occur at once. Time is indeed precious, no wonder the Bible records in ecclesiastics 3:1-8 "there is time for everything, and a season for every activity under the heavens: a time to be born and a time to die, a time to plant and a time to uproot, a time to kill and a time to heal, a time to tear down and a time to build, a time to weep and a time to laugh, a time to mourn and a time to dance, a time to scatter stones and a time to gather them, a time to embrace and a time to refrain from embracing, a time to search and a time to give up, a time to keep and a time to throw away, a time to tear and a time to mend, a time to be silent and a time to speak, a time to love and a time to hate, a time for war and a time for peace."

**Our deeds determine us as much as we
determine our deeds**

—George Elliott

According to Dr. J. Allan Petersen, "the finest gift we can give another human being is the gift of excellent expectation". Giving love to someone will always produce a reciprocal action from them; they give love back to you in whatever way they can, not just because they love you, but because in a way, you thought them to love and how to open their hand and eyes to love. Some may well oppose this by saying they have helped some people and they were repaid with evil by the same people they helped. Well, sometimes it happens I have been a victim severally, but think of it, are you helping them so that they will repay you someday? If you are thinking that way then you are not getting it right. Give for the joy of giving and for creating a space in your life for God's blessing. Even when you are hurt, betrayed or heartbroken, pardon them. That way, you will learn about trust and the significance of being careful to whom you open your heart to.

People need companionship and cheer every day, they needs someone whose thought are always correct to help them. People need someone kind to lend a helping hand, they need someone to gladly take the time to care and understand. People need someone to share each day to be a source of support. They want someone to give them courage when trouble comes no matter where they are, that is why God made us to love one another.

You need to be grateful for everyday and appreciate every moment and take from those moment everything that you possibly can, for you may be able to experience it again. Talk to people you have never talk to before and listen to what they have to say. Let yourself fall in love, break free and set your sight high. Hold your hand up because you have every right to. Tell yourself you are a great individual and believe in yourself, for if you don't believe in yourself it will be hard for others to believe in you. A friend said, "You can make everything you wish of life, create your own life, then go out and live it with absolute no regret. If you love someone tell him or her for you never know what tomorrow may have in store. Learn a lesson in life each day that you live. Today is the tomorrow you were worried about yesterday." Think about it was it worth it."

Monuments! What are they? The very pyramids have forgotten their builders or to whom they were dedicated. Deeds, not stones are the monument of the great.

—John L Motlex

Unarguably, one controvertible fact about life is that it can determine the course of events in your destiny. Have you ever evaluated any area of your life? If you live a productive life to impact positively to your generation, your deeds will orchestrate a chain of events that will work in your favor. Sometimes you may forget the good you did, but the good deeds cannot forget you. Always be mindful of this, what you have or what you have accomplished is not what really matters, but what matters is what you have done with those accomplishments, who have you helped with the little you have. Who have you made better with the much you have accomplished? If you don't help others, you will be hurting yourself. Whatever good you do comes back to you, it may not come immediately or just the way you did it, but it surely comes back to you may be in different way. Therefore, treat people the way you want people to treat you. I was told by my mother that this is the only important lesson in life, every other thing is commentary. If you desire to be happy; make people happy, it may cost you your time and resources, but you need to lose something you have so that you can become stronger than everything you lost. So if you want love; give out love in abundance, helping one another is what keeps people happy. You may not be able to change the bad things that happened to them, but you can change the sadness they have within them because of their past. They may be worried about the doctor's report against them, give them hope. Their boss may not like their faces, encourage them. My mentor called one day and said, "Johnson if someone treats you like animal just remember that there is something wrong with them, not you. Normal people don't go around destroying other human beings." Be willing to get whatever you give out. If you treat people like shit, they will treat you the same way some day.

Don't be afraid of doing good even if it meant being different from others, never leave someone who is stocked in life without helping them. Sometimes moving forward may no longer be desirable or achievable by your friend or relative, lend a helping hand, and give hope and encouragement, save a soul. In the order of men, certain rules are observed, but remember, God blesses us, not just for us only, but that we may be a blessing to others. Things must change for bigger things to materialize.

There's a story behind every person. There's a reason why they're the way they are. They aren't just like that because they want to. Something in the past created them, and sometimes it's impossible to fix them.

—J. Johnson

Let me refer you to the ignorance of this young boy with bad temper. There once was a little boy who had a bad temper. To make him stop his bad temper, his father gave him a bag of nail and told him that every time he lost his temper, he must hammer a nail into the back of the wall. The first day the boy had driven 37 nails into the wall. Over the next few weeks, as he learned to control his anger, the number of nails hammered daily gradually dwindled down. He discovered it was easier to hold his temper than to drive those nails into the wall.

Finally the day came when the boy didn't lose his temper at all. He told his father about it and his father suggested that he should pull out one nail for each day that he was able to hold his temper. The days passed and the boy was finally able to tell his father that the nails were gone; his father then took his son by the hand and led him to the wall and said, "You have done well my son, but look at the holes in wall. The wall will never be the same again. When you say something in anger, they leave a scar just like this one. You can put a knife in a man and draw it out, but it won't matter how many times you say "am sorry" the wound will still be there, a verbal wound is as bad as a physical one."

Have you been leaving a hole in someone's body? I was once told of a young lady who was hospitalized as a result of her anger on her husband because she thought her husband was unfaithful. She destroyed all the electronics in the house, as she rushed out of the house to destroy her husband's car; she was shot down by the security man who thought it was an armed robber. She was rushed to the hospital in a coma, her family and friends prayed continually that she come out of the coma and live. The coma continued for five days. The young lady finally awoke from the coma and said in perfectly lucid tones to her husband who was seated by her bed side "please forgive me, for my bad temper" and tears were seen flowing through the husbands chick as she slept and never woke up again. Think about it, how often have you been able to control your temper? Until you are able you control your temper, you may be losing precious opportunities.

To fall into a habit is to begin to cease to be

—Miguel De Unamuno

I once asked a group of people "being happy and being right, which do you prefer? Some said being right and others said they prefer to be happy, but a few of them who really took time to consider the implication of being "wrong" had trouble deciding. Peter McWilliams said "anything you abuse or overindulge in contributes to your negative thinking" This show that when you overdo a thing and you continue to do the same thing even if it's dangerous to you and you have no power or control over it to the degree that you begin to depend on it to cope with your daily life, you are addicted to it.

Negative thinking, smoking, alcohol abuse, drugs abuse, quick temper, compulsive sex, gossip, and many others that are not mentioned here are all habits which, eventually, become an obsession; they are all a kind of disease. Many people go through this malady because negative thinking is addictive to the mind, the body, and the emotions. If one doesn't get you, the others are waiting in the wings. A friend once told me that as a man you must do one of these things, (womanize, smoke and drink alcohol) he was so serious that he believes that every matured man must be doing one or more of these. But I told him I don't do any of that. Now does it mean am not a man? No, it's just that I refused to be abducted by them.

The mind is an awesome machine it is addicted to make right decision until you constantly drift away from it. Likewise the body is passionate to rush off chemicals poured into the blood stream by the voyage reply. That is why some people can resist the bodily stimulus of a serious session of unenthusiastic thoughts. They get off on the rush of adrenalin. Now the emotion on the other hand is captivated to the perpendicular force of it all. The wrestle or flight response may not activate enjoyable mind-set, but at least they are not boring. As the emotion becomes accustomed to a higher level of stimulation, they begin to demand more and more intensity and eventually, too much is no longer enough.

Negative thinking must be treated like any addiction—with commitment to life, patience, discipline, a will to get better, self love, and the knowledge that recovery is not just possible but following certain guidelines, inevitable.

There are two questions you must ask yourself: the first is 'who am I?' and the second is 'why am I here?' If these questions are in the wrong order you are in trouble

Permit me to draw your attention to what Anais Nin said. In one of her presentation to encourage friends, she said "Each friend represents a world in us, a world possibly not born until they arrive, and it is only by this meeting that a new world is born." You will agree with me that sometimes stranger come into your life, they become your friend and you have a feeling that they are meant to be there for you, to serve some sort of purpose, they teach you lessons or help you figure out who you are or who you are meant to be. You may not know who they are. They may be a roommate, a neighbor, a professor, a friend, a lover, or even a complete stranger, but somehow you will know that every moment they spent with you they affect your life in some positive way.

Sometimes they make you see things that happen to you that are horrible as mere challenges. Those challenges may be painful and unfair at first, but in reflection you find that without overcoming these obstacles you would have never realized your potentials strength and willpower. Be strong because Illness, injuries, lost moments of true greatness and share stupidity may occur to test the limit of your soul. Without these small tests, whatever they may be, life would be like a smoothly paved straight flat road to nowhere. It would be safe and comfort, but dull and utterly pointless.

More often people come to you and affect your life either positively or negatively, in fact sometimes you see people who are clueless about you judging you. Hear this, when you begin to experience this kind of thing, know that you are soon going to be a star. This is because it is an advertisement of some sort. Therefore, it absolutely depends on you to make use of the part they play or leave them. The accomplishment and downfall you experience helps you to create who you are and who you become. Even the bad experience can be learned from. In fact the bad experiences are sometimes the most important ones.

Let no corrupt communication proceed out of your mouth, but what is good for necessary edification, that it may impact grace to the hearers

—Ephesians 4:29

In very instructive and categorical terms, the spirit of God, through the Apostle Paul admonishes us not to engage in unwholesome or corrupt communication. Rather, the words that proceed out of our lips should be words that render healing to the broken heart, courage to the discouraged, and comfort to the afflicted.

James 2:3 a perfect man is one who doesn't offend in word. His words are consistent with God's word. When he speaks, his hearers are blessed, uplifted and edified. That is because his words are seasoned with grace.

Some people are so used to criticizing others instead of blessing and praying for them. Make a deliberate decision to keep away from destructive criticisms. Let your words be kind and affectionate, refuse to have itching ears for gossips, and don't company with those who are fond of discussing the affairs of others. Let your words concerning people be graceful, inspiring, motivating and encouraging.

Colossians 4:6 "let your speech be always with grace, seasoned with salt, that ye may know how ye ought to answer every man." I remember one of Joel Osteen's quotes which says "you can change your world by changing your words . . . remember, death and life are in the power of the tongue."

Many are yet to learn the important of words "Please", "excuse me", "am sorry", thank you" and appreciative words in their communication with others. They are of the erroneous belief that being polite is a sign of weakness in ones character, but that is not true. Rather, being polite is something that reveals the strength of character. In essence, when you use the right word to address others, you actually display the wisdom of God in you. Don't use bitter, harsh or abusive word in relating with those around you. Make sure that your communication encourages and inspires others positively.

If you must complain, complain to the people that matters

We seldom realize, for example that our most private thoughts and emotions should be controlled. Often times you hear people say Oh! I don't like the way I look! I don't like my stature, I am too thin, too short, too tall, too fat, too this, too that. People just worry about all these, although this is not only applicable to physique, but to other aspects of life such as finance, emotions, achieving goals, work, family, friends, and the lists goes on and on. Most people are never satisfied with what they have, they just want to be like the next person and the next person might actually want to be like them or someone else, hmmm, so sardonic! I once met a man, who told me that he sincerely wishes to be like me in future, then I asked him his age, in fact he was older than me. The rich complains and the poor complains, just imagine if human were God what do you think will happen? God created man in different ways. He made each and every one of us unique, but people complain so much that things began to fall apart. Relationships, marriages, families, jobs and so on. While most people are complaining, few people don't, because they know who they are. When you complain about everything in life you lose friends and faith, because there is no one who likes a complainer. It also hinders so many good things that are supposed to come to you. An illustration can be found in the Holy bible where the children of Israel complained about being brought from the land of Egypt to suffer, starve and die, that complain alone brought them 40 years of punishment by God which was wandering in the wilderness.

Before you complain or say any unkind words think of people who cannot even speak. Before you complain about the taste of your food think of someone who has nothing to eat. Before you complain about your spouse think of someone who is crying to God for a companion. Before you complain about your children think of people who desires children but don't have yet. Before you complain about how tired you are about your job think of the unemployed, the disabled and those who wish they had your job. Before you complain about life think of people who died earlier than expected. Complaining about things which we know cannot be changed will definitely not be changed, so refrain from those complains and proclaim the word God on those issues and begin to see challenges as blessing in disguise.

I'm not in Competition with anybody but myself.
My goal is to beat my last performance.

—Celine Dion

In my second book (*just imagine*) I wrote something about competition, how interesting it is to be involved in a healthy competition. Yesterday, a friend was telling me what he went through trying to compete with someone. He told me a short story about how he was jogging one day and he noticed someone a few distance in front of him, about seventy meters away, he said the man was running a little slower than him and he thought he will catch up with him. So he had few minutes to go his path before he needed to turn off and he started running faster and faster, he was coming closer to him just a little bit. After a few minutes he realized he was only a few meters away behind him. So he really picked up the pace and pushes the more. In fact you would have thought he was running in the last leg of London Olympic competition. He was determined to catch up with the man.

The more he tried the more difficult it becomes. Then finally he caught up with him and overtook him. This made him feel so good because he was able to achieve his desire, but one surprising thing is that after overtaking the man, he realized that the man doesn't even know about his struggle, so he was totally on his own. In fact he had gone six blocks past where he was supposed to stop. He had to turn around and get back.

This is what happens in life when we focus on competing with co-workers, neighbors, friends, family, trying to outdo them or trying to prove that we are more successful or more important? We spend our time and energy running after them and we miss out on our own paths to our God given destinies. The problem with unhealthy competition is that it is a never ending cycle. There will always be somebody ahead of you, someone with better job, nicer car, more money in the bank, more education, prettier wife, more handsome husband, better behaved children, etc. But realize that you can be the best that you can; you are not competing with no one. Some people are insecure because they pay too much attention to what others are doing, what others are saying, where others are going, what other are wearing & driving. Take what God has given you, the height, weight & personality. Dress well & wear it proudly! You'll be blessed by it.

Stay focused and lives your life well . . .

The truth is that stress doesn't come from your boss, your kids, your spouse, traffic jams, health challenges, or other circumstances. It comes from your thoughts about these circumstances.

—Andrew Bernstein

My father will always tell me to drive slowly so that I will get to my destination faster. I never knew what that meant until I saw this scenario. John saw it from afar and increased his speed just to beat the traffic with heartbeat racing and immediately, pandemonium of noise was heard as he applied the break, but then it was too late. His car had run uncontrollable to another car. Within few minutes the road was blocked, and it took the traffic police about two hours to clear the road. This was because John had refused to obey the traffic rules.

Traffic lights are designed not just to control the movement of car, but also to regulate the numbers of car and orderliness among road users. The lights which include green, orange and red representing "Go" "Ready" or "Be careful" and a "Stop" sign respectively. These ensure that road users adhering to these signs will get to their destination safety. Nevertheless some road users decide to take laws into their hand thinking they are wise, forgetting that they are endangering their lives and cars and also the lives and cars of other road users. Those traffic lights at various locations are placed by higher authority (Government) for good and vital purpose which is to control and maintain law and order of traffic on the road

If one can imagine a big town without traffic lights on their roads, try and paint a mental picture of what the scenario will look like: chaos, accidents, traffic jam and other unpleasant effects which are frustrating to the road users and society at large.

There are things which God has placed at various stages of your lives as traffic light but you sometimes ignore them by your thoughts, words and actions thereby causing chaos, frustrations, heartbreaks, failure etc. when you begin to adhere to those signs there will be peace and orderliness in your life and the people around you. In life there are traffic lights that you must obey to be successful. You must know when the light is green, orange and red. Knowing this will help you to move when you are supposed to move, to stop when you are supposed to stop and to get ready or be very careful when it is time for that. Praying to God for his guidance and direction will enable you to recognize and obey that "traffic light" which He has placed in your life.

It is possible to give away and become richer,
it is also possible to hold on too tightly and lose
everything. Yes, the liberal man shall be rich!
By watering others he waters himself

—Proverbs 11: 24-25

I like what Brain Sher said in one of his books, he said "if you want to be rich, don't try to make money, just add value to people's lives." This might look strange to some people, but it is ancient. Even the law of nature ensures you will end up getting more than what you have given out. You have only one life, why spend a day out without helping someone. Truth be told, it is not enough to live long; it's what you live for that truly matters. There are those who lived for more than a hundred years, but made no impact in the lives of those around them; nothing is significant about their lives. They really don't contribute to their society; always 'taking', never giving back.

Are you contributing positively to the advancement of the lives of those around you? This is a question you must ask yourself and truthfully answer. Chose to live a meaningfully life; one that will make the world move forward, touching the lives of others in a positive way. Be a blessing to others, and you will be lifted; you will be lifted as you lift others. Your promotion is in your promoting others. Your success is discovered when you help others discover theirs.

One of the fundamental principles of success is looking out for a human need, and reaching out to meet that need. A friend said "the best thing about giving ourselves is that what we get is always better than what we give. The reaction is greater than the action." When you consistently and consciously seek to improve your environment and make the world around you better than you met it, you will be a success. So always ask yourself "what can I do to improve my world" your world is your sphere of content, not just your world, but people around you. One attitude you must learn and always keep in mind is the giving attitude; it is a major key to success in life. Achievers mindsets are derived towards this. Don't accept the status quo. Be different and use your ideology to inspire people positively. Hoffer has this to say about helping others. "The pleasure we derive from doing favors is partly in the feeling it gives us that we are not altogether worthless. It is a pleasant surprise to us."

Three things that will always help you as you
journey through life.
One kindness
Two kindness
Three kindness.

A friend sent me a story of a poor boy who was begging from door to door to feed his hungry stomach; he decided to ask for a meal at next house. However, he lost his nerves when a lovely young girl opened the door. Instead of a meal, he asked for a glass of water. The girl thought he looked very hungry and weak, so she brought him a large glass of milk. He drank it slowly and asked thereafter. How much do I owe you? She replied. "You don't owe me anything, my mother thought us never to accept pay for any kindness." The boy said, "I thank you from the bottom of my heart, may God bless you". He walked away constantly looking back every three seconds as he fade away.

Many years later, that girl (now a woman) became critically ill and the local doctors tried their possible best to save her life, but they couldn't cure her. They finally sent her to the big city where specialists studied her rare illness more critically. Dr. Kelly was called for the consultation, when he heard the name of the town where the woman came from, a strange light filled his eyes. Immediately, he rose and went down the hall of the hospital to her room. He recognized her at once and he went back to the consultation room determined to do his best to save her life. From that day he gave special attention to her case. After a long struggle Dr. Kelly won and the woman was fine again. Dr. Kelly requested that her bill be passed to him for approval. He looked at the bill and wrote something on it as the woman open the bill she saw (paid in full) with a glass of milk. Tears filled her eyes as she immediately remembered. It is without doubt, people can give you pleasure, but the pleasure that keeps you going comes when others find pleasure though you. Whatever you have today is a function of opportunity placed before you to assist others. Your kindness goes far into the future to create opportunity for you. No wonder Winston Churchill said, "You make a living by what you get, but you make life by what you give."

Every form of kindness you show is never in vain, it reproduces itself. Well, it may not necessarily come the way you expected, but it always does. Always be kind every time all time.

**Some cause happiness where ever they go;
others whenever they go**

—Oscar Wilde

Natural circumstance may try to force you to believe that your business is the only means you can receive money, but refuse to let such a thought rule your life. Giving is God's established medium to prosper financially. Therefore, it doesn't matter how much you're paid for your job or your business. Never take that as your only source of income. It doesn't mean that you should handle your job with laxity. In fact do your job and business with excellence and shun mediocrity. "Work that you may have to give"

Some people believe that the reason they are suffering or poor is because of the kind of work they do. That's not true! The problem isn't the kind of job they do; rather it's in their mind and determination. Sometimes it is because they refuse to be kind to people.

Just Imagine J.K. Rowling, she wasn't even having a job; she was an unemployed single mother when she first started writing the Harry Potter series. She went on to sell more than 400 Million Harry Potter books in less than 10 years and has become a billionaire in the process. Many think that their success is hinged on making money through the hard work or getting employment, so they struggle and struggle till they get frustrated. When I was younger, I knew I would never be poor, not because my dad was rich, but because there were three things I had learnt to do properly; I could read and understand, I could cut hair and as time went on I learnt how to cut properly and I got better until I became convinced that if I had to be a barber, I will be the best, I learnt other trades. I know I could make good decision with logical reasoning. I read books about the rich and famous people like Ben Carson who struggled academically throughout elementary school and later became one of the best neurosurgeons of our time. I was constantly encouraged by people like Bill Gate who didn't even complete university education, but went on to develop his interest in computer programming.

In fact his wealth index in 1998 reveals that Bill Gate was so rich that if he dropped a $1,000 bill on the ground, it was just not worth his time to bend over and pick it up. With these in my mind daily I was motivated and I knew I would be great. You must look beyond your job, think of what you can do to help people, that way you will be a great and a better person.

Happy are those who faces challenges, they are more responsible, for life without challenges is life without success

Isn't it amazing that we often approach life imagining that we are in some sort of competition with others? We often hate and envy people for what they have eluded us. We often get angry and bitter on account of other peoples accomplishments. We often fight and struggle for positions. We often get caught up in an unhealthy rivalry and competition because we feel disadvantaged.

Hear this, there is a place for each one and there is an opportunity for everyone. There is future for everyone as well as a helper for everyone. Don't break your head when it seems someone has gotten an opportunity, don't lose sleep because someone got a job or a car. Don't sulk in despair when it seems all your mates have gone ahead of you. It's only a matter of time. The same God who got a place for others will do it for you.

The height you seek may seem unattainable, but God can connect you within a minute. Don't feel dejected when it seems your strength is not enough. Remember, when cable News Network (CNN) first appeared in 1980, its competitors derided it as Chicken Noodle Network, but twenty years later CNN is American's number one network for news and has emerged as a global brand. So don't give up at every good work you do. You may think that you are going through hell, no you are not. In fact Bertrand Russell in one of his encouraging speech said you should if you have to. He said "if you are going through hell, keep going".

Yes, it's true that sometimes you stray into distressing situations and you can't bring yourself out. Sometimes you take bad decisions that threaten to consume you, sometime you slip into dangerous addictions and you can't find your way out. And other times you get into a financial mess and you have no means of coming out. Some families, marriages, career, businesses, academics etc often slips into crises and they often have no idea on how to pull out. Hear this, hang on, help is on the way. There is always something in you that is greater than that little idea telling you to quit. Therefore, decide and use this time to make a newer choice for a newer life.

Never forget the three powerful resources you always have available with you: Love, Prayer and Forgiveness.

H. Jackson Brown, Jr.

Prayers are observed in different ways. In fact sometimes people discriminate how other people pray, you even find the discrimination within people of the same religion and the same faith. They do this because they feel others are not praying their own way and therefore they are wrong. Read what Mahatma Gandhi said about prayer "Prayer is not asking. It is a longing of the soul. It is daily admission of one's weakness. It is better in prayer to have a heart without words than words without a heart."

Well, the good thing is that prayer can be a wish, a whisper, a sign, a meditation, a thank you or "I am sorry" to God, prayer is characterize by praise, faith, anticipation, authority and thanksgiving. It means communication with God; it is like communicating with a friend, father, mother, sister, brother or close acquaintance. Communicating with God does not have to be said perfectly like a recitation, but as long as it comes from one's heart with belief and thanksgiving that it is going to be answered. Some prayers are not answered immediately, especially when the person is praying amiss—that is, not praying for the needed or relevant things and God knowing that the things you ask for will either mar or destroy you if given to you; He withholds from you such extravagant wealth, promotion and so on. It is like in a family where a father will not give everything requested for but makes sure he provides the necessary or basic needs for the child.

Nevertheless prayer is the ultimate key to everything in life, praying to Almighty God means communicating with Him every day; this is because there is no individual who does not communicate with other individual every day. When you don't pray to God, He may not answer your exact needs. On the cross at the point of death, Jesus Christ still prayed to God.

As a result, whatever situation you should pray to God to give Him thanks for the things He has done, for the things is doing, for the things He is yet to do and for the thing He will not do. We pray not because prayer is powerful, but because the God we pray to is powerful. Robert Frost said "Forgive me my nonsense as I also forgive the nonsense of those who think they talk sense."

Let no one weep for me, or celebrate my funeral with morning; for I still live, as I pass to and fro through the mouths of men

—Quintus Ennius

Last week I was discussing with a man of about 60 years and suddenly the issue of death came up and I asked him sir, when would you like to die? You can't believe his reaction. In fact he advised that we should just end the conversation, but the truth is that death is real. So I ended up with this quote by Steve Jobs you may have read it, he said "No one wants to die. Even people who want to get to heaven don't want to die to get there. And yet death is the destination we all share. No one has ever escaped it. And that is as it should be, because death is very likely the single best invention of life. It is life's change agent. It clears out the old to make way for the new."

Generally, people fear death. They will do anything humanly possible to keep this enemy from snatching their lives. However, mankind has not been able to avoid death. Most times people are so fearful about death that they fear to take some risk which may even give them better life. Some fear death so much because they think it brings some kind of separation from their loved ones, places and things. Yes, death may separate you from your people, but it does not separate your eternal value, they will remain with you forever. Do you have any eternal value to look up to in heaven if death comes calling now? Everyone knows that they are going to die some day; every one of us knows that. The truth is, none of us believe it because if we did, we will do things differently.

The irony is that a lot of times, only when we learn how to die then we learn how to live. I know it may sound very morbid to you, but it's the truth—that is why you must do what you have to do now. A lot of people are ruin by allowing the society, media and friends to dictate for them how to live

Not according to what other people tell you to do; you have to decide whether you want to serve yourself, whether you are going to make a difference in somebody else's life or just exit.

Most importantly, I think true joy comes from knowing God. Not just knowing about God because you can read the bible to know about God and not knowing God personally; So to sum it up, the earlier you sort out the priorities in your lives, the better you live.

Do not let spacious plans for a new world divert your energies from saving what is left of the old.

Winston Churchill

It has been observed that in life we often make plans on how things will work for us, only for our plans to collapse like a pack of cards. We habitually figure out how we will achieve all we want to achieve, but sometimes things just refused to work as we planned. We frequently make fantastic plans by human standards, but for some startling reasons they don't work the way we would have wished. As much as possible, observation must be done before planning. Observation helps you to think and plan without making mistakes.

Hear this!

When your plans and it fails don't relent, plan again, again and again. You will get to where you want to be sooner if you do not quit. Napoleon Hills said "when defeat comes, accept it as a signal that your plans are not sound, rebuild these plans, and set sail once more towards your coveted goal." When you exhaust your options without results, then run to God He has more than enough plans that will bring the desire of your heart.

Of a truth, sometimes the things that will lead you to your desired result often seem boring and tedious? It seems tiresome to pray repeatedly, it seems very hard to live a righteous life every day, believe God by faith every day and go to work every day. Just hang on. Your effort may seems monotonous, but soon you will witness results if you do not quit, be consistent in your career, business, ministry, family and academics. There is a massive harvest just by the door.

When making your plan, do things that will make you happy, whatever makes you happy, as long as it doesn't hurt you or someone else and it is not a sin, please go on and do it. It is important that you make your schedules or plan pleasurable by adding enjoyable activities into your life with the same dedication, precision and precedence. In your plan, try making a list of the things you enjoy doing, pursue them and do them often to create a constant happiness. I am yet to see anyone who makes plan to be a failure, a dull person, a poor person or a fool. In fact these things come when you refuse to make plans and work towards your plan.

You have to motivate yourself with challenges, that's how you know that you're still alive

—Jerry Seinfeld

Friends, have you noticed that many time people tend to forget their root and even the God they worship when faced with crises. They fail to stand on what they believe and understand about God. Often times circumstances makes you forget all that you have learnt and know about God when you are on the hot seat of destiny. Do you know why the devils desire to make you forget everything you ever heard about God when you need it most? The reason is simple:

No one is immune from share of challenges, but understanding is your first weapon in the battle of life, understanding who you are and your advantage over the enemy or what it is you are battling with. Even when the battle seems to be against you; you must stand up and fight back. Most people are faced with different challenges in life and in trying to overcome these challenges they end up causing more harm than good. You don't turn to drug or alcohol when you are facing great challenges. If you always depend on drugs and alcohol to live, then you are using them negatively and you invite more pain to yourself. One of the things we hate most as human being is pains.

Pain hurts, that is why we try to do almost anything we can to avoid pain. So if truly we do not want pains, why do you continue to do things you know will result mental or physical pain? George Bernard Shaw said "people are always blaming their circumstances for what they are; I don't believe in circumstances, the people who get on this world are the people who get up and look for the circumstances they want, and, if they can't find them, make them." So if what you are facing is not what you want, change it anyhow and create what you want, make yourself happy not by adding to your trouble. Whatever it is that is causing you pain, it is time to get up and be strong. You must not continue to live with pain. Don't think that feeling bad and getting worried will change your situation. No, it won't you must get up and tell yourself that you are not created for pain; you are made to be happy, be strong and refuse to stay on those circumstances. Above all, seek and grow in understanding by studying Gods word.

We now live in a world full of illusion, where people are greatly misled, values are thrown away and impiety are embraced

Obviously, the things that are dear to us easily become the subject of attack and we tend to do everything to protect them. The things that are precious to us become a target for the enemy. The things that we don't want to lose often become the prime target that the enemy wishes to steal. When the enemy chooses to attack, he goes for the things we love and value. Instead of attacking our liabilities, the enemy attacks our assets. Is there an area of your life that has repeatedly become a subject of attack?

Whatever the enemy is fighting against is a treasure you must begin to treat with a measure of importance. When the devil fights your relationship with God, it's a sign of how important that relationship is. If it's your prayer life, it is because a magnitude of blessing is coming your way if you keep praying. If you are attacked by the devil, that is simply because you are important and every attack by the enemy shall be futile. The devil is now using government official to deny people their legitimate right. They torture the citizens they are supposed to serve and protect.

A man while in government service made sure that he embezzled the public fund within his reach, knowing that his retirement is coming up soon. He sold most of the government properties and converted the money to his own. He hid the money in a corner of his underground bungalow and went continually to visit and inspect it. This arouse the curiosity of his workmen who suspected that there was a treasure there, when his masters back was turned he went to the spot, and stole everything. When the man returned and found the place empty, he wept and tore his hair, but a neighbor who saw him in his extravagant grief learned the cause of it, said; fret thyself no longer, but take a stone and put it in the same place and think it is your money for as you never meant to use it, the one will do you as much as the other. The worth of money is not in possessing it, but in using it not just for you alone, but to help the people around you. How have you possessed your wealth and how are you using it? I keep telling my friends who find it difficult to really invest their money. Money can be kept in the bank, but that is not what money is meant for.

"If you have a goal, write it down.
If you do not write it down, you do not have a goal,
you have a wish."

—Steve Maraboli

I was teaching some group of young students who are yet to make decision with their lives, and I asked them, "how many of you love to read books?" a few hand were up, and I asked again, "how many of you love to watch TV?" all hands were up, and I asked again, "how many of you love to read book more than they love to watch TV?" and just two hands were up. Again, I asked them "how many of you wishes to be great?" all hands were up. I told them that the truth is this, those of you who like to read book more than they love to watch TV, will always be more successful in their academic.

I love this great saying "If wishes were horses, poor men would ride them and most people would have big stables." Everyone wishes for something no matter the age young or old, but most wishes are human desires and when those desires are fed on they eventually turn in wishes. We wish for how our events could have been amended in the past, what we want to happen now and how, what and where things should or are suppose to happen, but they don't go the way we want them. Humans always want more, they wish to have money, but what they really want is to be carefree, they wish to have power while what they really want is control, they wish to have beauty while what they really want is love, sometimes they know it, sometimes they don't.

Do you wonder why God doesn't grant all your wishes immediately, to grant all of man wishes is to take away his ambitions, purpose and dreams, because life is only worth living if you have something to thrive for and to aim at. Thank God that God doesn't punish immediately for all our mistakes. We should never wish for wishful thinking because there is no point having if you don't try to do them, it is just like faith without works is dead. While reflecting on life and human experiences Steve Maraboli said "Do not dilute the truth of your potential.

We often convince ourselves that we cannot change, that we cannot overcome the circumstances of our lives. That is simply not true. You have been blessed with immeasurable power to make positive changes in your life. But you can't just wish it, you can't just hope it, you can't just want it . . . you have to LIVE it, BE it, DO it." It is time to stop dreaming, and do something about the dream, you need to know what you need in life and go for it.

I struggle to comprehend this; the point of being
pretty on the outside when the inside
is so ugly and putrid.

I was having a breakfast with a friend who recently celebrated her 40th birthday at the Marina bay in Singapore and suddenly she reminded me about a quote in Gorge MacDonald's book where David Elginbrod speaks to those who wonder, at times, why God has made them the way they are—and who wish they were someone else. Read what these two were busy saying. Lady Emily Muses: "I wish I were you Margret." Margret answers: if I were you my lady, I would rather be what God chose to make me than the most glorious creature that I could think of. For to have been thought about-born in God's thoughts-and then made by God, is the dearest, not most precious thing in all thinking" it's a comforting thought to know that we are not a terrible mistake, but a very special creation born in God's thoughts. That's the reason I opine with David when he says I am fearfully and wonderfully made. In fact people spent a lot of money to recreate their looks and this of course doesn't stop them from being who they are right within them, the case of Jian Feng is one you must glean from. In 2012 a man from northern China, Jian Feng sued his wife for being ugly. Jian was very shocked by the child's appearance and this made him angry with his wife not because she was really ugly, but because she had spent over $60,000 dollars on plastic surgery before they got married and she did not tell her husband. Well, the man got to know after their daughter's birth who neither looked like the man nor her wife, but ugly (that is looking like the wife, how she really was) and sued her for being ugly. Well, you may ask "what is wrong with plastic surgery?" some people do it to regain a normal look after an accident (which is understandable) and others do it to correct superficial blusher flaws. However you look at it, plastic surgical procedure has serious disadvantages which includes, health impediment, sever hemorrhage, infection, nerve damage and many more. In fact the worst is that you are telling God that you don't like they way He made you. You must appreciate yourself the way you are because you are original. Permit me to introduce you to this great man, Nike Vujicic, he is a man without arms and leg, yet you hardly see him without smiles on his face. Even in his situation he appreciates God the way he is, in fact he goes round the world encouraging people to love God and be grateful.

The problem with most people is they sow bad seeds in the night; then they go to church in the morning and pray to reap good crops

I like Albert Einstein's quote on sowing and reaping, he said *"keep on sowing your seed, for you never know which will grow-perhaps it all will."* It is possible that somewhere in the world right now a farmer is dropping seeds into the ground and pretty soon those seeds will begin to change the place where they were planted. The carefully prepared soil that looks hard today will soon become a field ready for harvest tomorrow. In fact no one to my knowledge argues the law of sowing and reaping. A farmer who sows wheat is never surprise when wheat begins to grow from the ground where it was planted. That's the universal law of sowing and reaping. In the same way, sowing happens to be a choice, one may decide to or not to saw. Similarly, you may also decide what to sow and what not to sow; the choice of crop you sow is precisely the crop you reap.

As a farmer you must be careful of the kind crops you sow, because it's an investment which you must reap accordingly. If you plant cassava there is no how you are going to reap yam no matter how hard you wish to get yam. What you sow is what you will reap. Another interesting thing about sowing and reaping is that whatever you sow does not sprout overnight, they take time to germinate and you reap in different season in plenty. I am in agreement with Mark Twain when he said, "twenty years from now you will be more disappointed by the things that you didn't do than by the ones you did do. So throw off the bowlines. Sail away from the safe harbor. Catch the trade winds in your sails, Explore, Dream and Discover."

Frankly, if you plant kindness, you will reap kindness, if you plant love, you will reap love. And one good thing about reaping is that you get more than you sow; that is to say, if you sow wickedness, you will get it in abundance and if you sow kindness, you will also get kindness in great quantity. However, if you refuse to sow, then you will get nothing in abundance. This shows that there are consequences in everything you do. Many people today make choices without considering the result and most times the choices they made and act on destroys them and others too. The law of sowing and reaping is there to help you understand that every choice and action you take has a consequence. So think about it, what kind of crops have you been sowing?

Life has three rules.
First, love your maker and how you are made
Second, be a giver
Third, always remember the first.

While on a vacation in Cyprus, I attended a modest country church in Nicosia. Having taken the hymns, I did not enjoy the hymns as I should, probably because of my experiences with good singing. Then a godly pastor mounted the pulpit and faithfully taught the word of God. He started by reading the book of Matthew 7:12 "therefore all things whatsoever ye would that men should do to you, do ye even so to them: for this is the law and the prophet." Right now I can still remember the seriousness on the pastor's face as he preached the gospel with passion and love.

He then concluded with a story. He said "a boy and his father were walking on the mountains. Suddenly the boy was hurts and he screamed: "Aaah!!!" To his surprise, he hears the voice repeating, somewhere in the mountain: "Aaah!!! Curious, he yells: "Who are you?" He receives the answer: "Who are you?" Angered at the response, he screams: "Coward!" He receives the answer: "Coward!" He looked at his father and asked: "What's going on?" The father smiles and says: "My son, pay attention." And then he screams to the mountain: "I admire you!" The voice answers: "I admire you!" Again the man screams: "You are a champion!" The voice answers: "You are a champion!" The boy was surprised, but did not understand. Then his father said: "People call this ECHO, but really this is LIFE. It gives you back everything you say or do. Our life is simply a reflection of our actions." If you want more love in the world, create more love in your heart. If you want more competence in your team, improve your competence. This relationship applies to everything, in all aspects of life; Life will give you back everything you have given to it.

More than this, however, you must keep in mind that whatever you do, you will always get the result. If you are good to people, you will get good result and if you do bad you will get bad result. If you believe in doing good, stand by it and don't be afraid for what you believe in, even if you have to stand alone.

Happiness cannot be traveled to, owned, earned, or worn. It is the spiritual experience of living every minute with love, grace & gratitude.

—Denis Waitley

A friend forwarded a life provoking story of a lady to me and after reading I begin to imagine how irrational human can be sometimes. The story goes thus; "a young lady was waiting for her flight in the boarding room of a big airport. As she would need to wait many hours, she decided to buy a book to spend her time. She also bought a packet of cookies. She sat down in an armchair, in the VIP room of the airport, to rest and read in peace. Beside the armchair where the packet of cookies lay, a man sat down in the next seat, opened his magazine and started reading. When she took out the first cookie, the man took one also.

She felt irritated but said nothing. She just thought: "What a nerve! If I was in the mood I would punch him for daring!" For each cookie she took, the man took one too. This was infuriating her but she didn't want to cause a scene. When only one cookie remained, she thought: "ah . . . What would this abusive man do now?" Then, the man, taking the last cookie, divided it into half, giving her one half. Ah! That was too much! She was much too angry now! In a huff, she took her book, her things and stormed to the boarding place.

When she sat down in her seat, inside the plane, she looked into her purse to take her eyeglasses, and to her surprise, her packet of cookies was there, untouched, unopened! She felt so ashamed! She realized that she was wrong . . . She had forgotten that her cookies were kept in her purse. The man had divided his cookies with her, without feeling angered or bitter. "While she had been very angry, thinking that she was dividing her cookies with him. And now there was no chance to explain, or to apologize." There are 4 things that you cannot recover: The stone . . . after the throw! The word . . . after it's said! The occasion . . . after the loss! The time . . . after it is gone."

As such, you need to cherish every moment and fill it with love. Show love with whoever you meet today because you may not meet them again tomorrow.

107

Start by doing what's necessary, then what's possible; and suddenly you are doing the impossible.

—Saint Francis of Assisi

Stephen Covey told a story as he tries to motivate people to work. He said "once upon a time, a very strong woodcutter asked for a job in a timber merchant and he got it. The pay was really good and so was the work condition. For those reasons, the woodcutter was determined to do his best. His boss gave him an axe and showed him the area where he supposed to work. The first day, the woodcutter brought eighteen trees. "Congratulations," the boss said. "Go on that way!" Very motivated by the boss words, the woodcutter tried harder the next day, but he could only bring fifteen trees. The third day he tried even harder, but he could only bring ten trees. Day after day he was bringing less and less trees. "I must be losing my strength", the woodcutter thought. He went to the boss and apologized, saying that he could not understand what was going on. "When was the last time you sharpened your axe?" the boss asked. "Sharpen? I had no time to sharpen my axe. I have been very busy trying to cut trees." This reflects that our lives are like that. We sometimes get so busy that we don't take time to sharpen the "axe". In today's world, it seems that everyone is busier than ever, but less happy that ever. Could it be that we have forgotten how to stay "sharp"?

As optimistic as this, there is nothing wrong with activity and hard work. But you should not get so busy that we neglect the most important things in life, like your personal life, taking time to get close to your Creator, giving more time for your family, taking time to read etc. We all need time to relax, to think and meditate, to learn and grow. If you don't take the time to sharpen the "axe", you will become dull and lose our effectiveness.

While you live remember that all the art of existence lies in a fine mingling of checks and balance. While you are very busy working, you most always stop and check your "axe". Driving a

109

car without maintenance will certainly break down on the road some day. In the same way, human is made of the body, soul and spirit, as such, eating normal food without spiritual food will certainly breakdown the body some day. Watch yourself are you just working? Do you constantly check your working "Axe"?

"When I was in grade school, they told me to write down what I wanted to be when I grew up. I wrote down happy. They told me I didn't understand the assignment, I told them they didn't understand life"

—anonymous

People are convinced that life will be better after they get married, have kids, buy cars, but soon they are frustrated that the kids aren't old enough and that they'll be more content when they are grown. After that, they're frustrated that they have teenagers to deal with. They'll certainly be happy when they're out of that stage. They tell their selves that their lives will be complete when their spouse gets his or her act together, when they get a nicer car, when they are able to go on a nice vacation, and suddenly when we retire. The truth is, there's no better time to be happy than right now. If not now, when? Your life will always be filled with challenges and those challenges make you who you are. It's best to admit this to yourself and decide to be happy anyway. One of my favorite quotes comes from Alfred D. Souza. He said, "For a long time it had seemed to me that life was about to begin—real life. But there was always some obstacle in the way, something to be gotten through first, some unfinished business, time still to be served, or a debt to be paid. Then life would begin. At last it dawned on me that these obstacles were my life."

This perspective has helped me to see that there is no way to happiness. Happiness is the way. So, treasure every moment that you have and treasure it more because you shared it with someone special, special enough to spend your time with . . . and remember that time waits for no one.

So, stop waiting . . . until you finish school, until you go back to school, until you lose ten pounds, until you gain ten pounds, until you have kids, until your kids leave the house, until you start work, until you retire, until you get married, until you get divorced, until Friday night, until Sunday morning, until you get a new car or home, until your car or home is paid off.

There is no better time than right now to be happy! I have learnt so much from my mistakes . . . I'm thinking of making a few more that is why each day when I wake up I thank God and I tell myself I will make myself happy, no one is capable of stealing my happiness. Not man, not my job, not my friends, not even the challenges of the day. I will always make me happy because I have the power to do so today.

Life's challenges are not supposed to paralyze you;
They're supposed to help you discover who you are.

—Bernice Johnson

The story of this donkey and its owner was gleaned from a friends work on encouragement and hope. He said "one day a farmer's donkey fell down into a well. The animal cried piteously for hours as the farmer tried to figure out what to do. Finally, he decided the animal was old, and the well needed to be covered up anyway; it just wasn't worth it to retrieve the donkey. He invited all his neighbors to come over and help him. They all grabbed a shovel and began to shovel dirt into the well. At first, the donkey realized what was happening and cried horribly. Then, to everyone's amazement, he quieted down.

A few shovel loads later, the farmer finally looked down the well. He was astonished at what he saw. With each shovel of dirt that hit his back, the donkey was doing something amazing. He would shake it off and take a step up. As the farmer's neighbors continued to shovel dirt on top of the animal, he would shake it off and take a step up. Pretty soon, everyone was amazed as the donkey stepped up over the edge of the well and happily trotted off!.."

Having read this, it reflects that "life is going to shovel dirt on you, all kinds of dirt. The trick to getting out of the well is to shake it off and take a step up. Each of our troubles is a steppingstone. You can get out of the deepest wells just by not stopping, never giving up! Shake it off and take a step up. Remember the five simple rules to be happy: 1. Free your heart from hatred—Forgive. Two. Free your mind from worries—Most never happens, three. Live simply and appreciate what you have. Four. Give more. Five. Expect less from people but more from yourself".

Sorry means you feel the pulse of other people's pain as well as your own, and saying it means you take a share of it. Sorry is the wake of misdeed. It's the crippling ripple of consequence. Sorry is a question that begs forgiveness, because the metronome of a good heart won't settle until things are set right and true.

—Craig Silvey,

When he realized all that he had done, he decided to travel back home to his family to apologize especially to his father. Edward was on a flight to see his family after squandering his money and life on alcohol and drugs, he went to prison for drug possession. He was later granted pardon, and so he went back home. Before he left his home, Edward always had arguments with his father, due to his extravagant and unnecessary spending, drugs and womanizing but he always claimed he was a grown man, shouted at his father and always walked out on his father during the arguments. His mother pleaded with him to apologize to his father and tell him how sorry he was for his actions but he never did. Now, he had sobered up and was ready to tell his family how sorry he was, especially to his father. But it was too late to say sorry because his father passed away the previous day due to hypertension and stroke. Edward cried so much that he wished he could turn back the hands of time, and he could tell his father how sorry he was for everything that had happened before and after he left. I remember Claire London as she chronicles her effort to tackle this; she said "I have learned that sometimes "sorry" is not enough sometimes you actually have to change."

Sorry is a simple five letter word to say, but most times the hardest to say when it matters the most. We all know that saying sorry is a simple solution to most situations but saying sorry is so hard for some people and this is due to pride and over confidence. Saying sorry does not really take out a hair out of you, nor does it take your money or energy. You may even lose your friends, families or integrity when we don't say it. Whenever King David transgressed against God, he was always sorry and prayed for forgiveness even when it costs him something (2 Samuel 12 vs16-18) Sorry is a debt repaid, it is a question that begs forgiveness, metronome of a good heart that won't settle until things are set right and true. Sorry doesn't take things back, but it pushes things forward and it bridges a gap. Now think again, are there people you need to say sorry to?

Never cut a tree down in the wintertime. Never make a negative decision in the low time. Never make your most important decisions when you are in your worst moods. Wait. Be patient. The storm will pass. The spring will come.

—Robert H. Schuller

Yesterday as we were about to round up the annual youth conference, the last speaker was talking on patience, she told us a story and I was greatly moved. Permit me to share this with you. She said "A dog was so faithful that her owner could leave her baby with it and go out to attend other matters. She always returned to find the child soundly asleep with the dog faithfully watching over him. One day something tragic happened. The woman as usual, left the baby in the "hands" of this faithful dog and went out shopping. When she returned, she discovered rather a nasty scene, there was a total mess. The baby's cot was dismantled; his nappies and clothes torn to shreds with blood stains all over the bedroom where she left the child and the dog. Shocked, the woman wailed as she began looking for the baby. All of a sudden, she saw the faithful dog emerging from under the bed.

It was covered with blood and licking its mouth as it had just finished a delicious meal. The woman went berserk and assumed that the dog had devoured her baby. Without much thought she beat the dog to death. But as she continued searching for the

"remains" of her baby, she beheld another scene. Close to the bed was the baby who, although lying on bare floor, was safe.

Under the bed the body of a snake torn to pieces in what must have been a fierce battle between it and the dog which was now dead. Then reality dawned on the woman who now began to understand what took place in her absence. The dog fought to protect the baby from the ravenous snake, but she got killed by the woman. Now it was too late for her to make amends because in her impatience and anger, she had killed the faithful dog."

How often have you misjudged people and torn them to shreds with harsh words and deeds before you have had time to evaluate the situation? Presuming things your way without taking the trouble to find out exactly what the situation really is. Little patience can drastically reduce major lifelong mistakes. Who are you misjudging right now? Don't think what others are thinking." When she ended the story a lot of youths were shedding tears. Can you imagine how many people you may have murdered with your mouth alone?

It was pride that changed angels into devils; it is humility that make men as angels

—Saint Augustine

As an important paradigm for success you must be careful with pride when considering the sheer size of your accomplishment. Pride is associated with elated gratification and feeling of achievement. Truth be told, there is nothing wrong in being wealthy, however everything is wrong when you begin to take the glory to yourself and forgetting God who gave you the power to make wealth. Watch it. Your action, reaction and feeling when you help other may trigger pride. Pride can be seen in two different ways. First as a virtue, this is when you have the feeling to achieve knowing who you are. The greatness in your mind to acknowledge who you are and what you believe in. Secondly, pride can be seen as a vice that can lead to total vanity, thereby bringing destruction of life and its accomplishments.

You must have a common understanding of pride that result to vanity, self-directed satisfaction, disproportionate self esteem and egotism. Before his exit, Steve Jobs viewed pride as something that will make you late. He said "Remembering that I'll be dead soon is the most important tool I've ever encountered to help me make the big choice in life. Because almost everything—all expectations, all pride, all fear of embarrassment and failure— these things just fall away in the face of death, leaving only what is truly important." Again, watch yourself if you have been too proud of what you have and who you are. Saint Augustine said in his teaching that "It was pride that changed angels into devils; it is humility that makes men as angels. As such you must humble yourself in whatever you do and wherever you are.

One thing about pride is that sometimes you may be that last person to notice that you are proud. You may even feel you are doing the right thing, when you help people how do you do that? What are your intensions, to be notice? To be praised? You need to steer clear of pride because it is able of eroding all your excellent work. You neglect God when you adorn any attribute of pride, even if you singlehandedly build a village with good works, but you are proud, people will see your pride more than your good works. As such, your pride has spoilt your years of good work because you are seen as competition with God. Think about it have you been proud in any way?

He that is of the opinion money will do everything may well be suspected of doing everything for money

—Benjamin Franklin

Do you need money or you are just worried about it? A quote says "worrying is the interest paid on a debt you may not owe". When you worry about money you become afraid, fear leads to anxiety and you become anxious about feeding, clothes, house, cars, and so on. Have you ever asked yourself "what are the basic needs of life?" these basic needs for man's existence includes air, water, shelter, food and clothing. God has provided them freely from the origin of time. With or without money human beings have been around and survived for a long time Matthew 6:25-34 "Therefore take no thought saying 'what shall we eat or what shall we drink or wherewithal shall we be clothed? "For your heavenly Father knoweth that ye have need of all these things.

Do you need money? Of course we need money to get our needs, when you worry about money every time and make it, master of thoughts, actions, speeches and your life, you are invariably, money's slave and you will definitely do anything to get it. For the love of money is the root of all evil, which while some coveted after, they have erred from the faith and pierced themselves through with many sorrows. When you know what you need or want, you won't worry so much about money. Most people don't know what they want, they think they know but they really don't, know. Having lists of things you need will help you set your goals.

Before you worry about money ask yourself whether you truly need the things you are worried about. Remember the saying: "Money isn't everything It can buy you a bed but not sleep, It can buy you a clock but not time, It can buy you a book but not knowledge, It can buy you a position but not respect, It can buy you medicine but not health, It can buy you blood but not life, It can buy you sex but not love."

Work like you don't need the money, love like you've never been hurt and dance like no one is watching

—Randell G. Leighton

The priest just mounted the pulpit and having said prayers, he started with a short story that made me have a rethink. He said he was driving home one day and there was a heavy traffic which held all vehicles for few minutes under the falling snow. As they slowly drove through the pathway he noticed an old man trying to cross the road and he was waving his long walking stick so that the cars would stop for him to cross, but a lot motorist ignored the old man. So he stopped his car in the middle of the road and helped the old man cross the road. As he turned to pick his car, the old man said "can you give me some money please?" now the priest became stunned and angry for a moment because he was expecting "a thank you" from the old man, instead of thanks the old man was asking for more. Well, the priest eventually gave him some money, but he went away wondering what kind of ungrateful old man was he.

Finally, as he was driving home he thought about the incident and a solemn voice whispered to him saying "Son, this is how am treated often." And immediately he prayed and asks God to forgive him. Think about it, have you loved money so well that you find it difficult to give out your money? When Henry Ford was speaking to a group of businessmen he said "a business that makes nothing but money is a poor business" if you really want to win people's heart, or impart them positively you must give. Little kindness with money is often worth more than a thousand of preaching. Some people fine it easier to render any help, but when it has to do with giving money they are not path of it. Having realized his shortcoming, the priest said, "Why should I get angry over such little favor?" continually you receive from God, most times, you don't even thank Him for the past blessing and you immediately ask for another blessing. Yet He looks at you with mercy and blesses you again. Therefore, if they are not appreciative of your kindness to them, move on, don't stop blessing other people.

**You only live once, but if you do it right,
once is enough**

—Mae West

It has been almost eight years since I traveled through this road, but at this spot I remembered how it all happened and some goose pimple were all over me again. "Sometime in April, I was traveling from one state to another for a business trip, I boarding a popular transit bus. The journey started smoothly, but after about one hour twenty minutes just about thirty minutes before a nearby city we saw some vehicle stopping and passenger running into the bush. We also stopped and ran into the bush. We were there for more than one hour until we learnt that the armed robbers are gone. They were dangerously armed according to a victim who was badly injured. The armed robber instructed them to Place all their money on the floor and told them never to play pranks because they'll be searched. While other robbers (a mix of male and female) were offloading all the passenger's bags into their own van, three were collecting the money seat by seat. They also searched and make them to lie down on the floor.

Then something happened. There was a young woman in her 20's who was dressed in all black. She had a baby in her arms. She was seated next to another older woman. When the robbers struck, this young lady quickly split her money into two and hid some in her baby's pampers as she dropped the rest on the floor.

The man said that there was another older woman who was also seating in the same row with them. The woman saw this young lady as she hide part of her money. When they got to her, they told her to drop the baby and stand for a search. She did that and they found nothing on her; they looked at her baby and asked her to sit down.

The thieves were leaving and suddenly, the woman seated next to the nursing mother screamed "She hid money in her baby's pampers". The robber lifted the baby up and tore her pampers, they removed the money and shot the baby and they left.

The baby's mother fainted. The passengers immediately hit the woman who reported to death and they left her body on the road. Please think with me. Man's inhumanity to man. This is man that is created to love one another.

It is not amazing that with money you can get things done, what is amazing is using limited life to chase unlimited money

As she came back to desk to continue with her work, Anne saw a carefully wrapped gift on her desk. She was so surprised that she quickly unwrapped it to see what it was and who the giver was. She was thrilled when she saw the name of the sender written on the inner cover of the gift; she never expected that Jenny would ever remember her again. With tears of joy she picked up her phone to make calls.

Ordinarily when a person receives a gift from another person, the receiver is pleased. The gift will be treasured especially if it is a unique gift from a loved one whenever it is seen or remembered. Above all, if it is gifts from God. Gifts bring smile not just to the face of the receiver, but also to the face of the giver. Gifts from men are temporary, perishable or fades with time, but gifts from God are eternal, priceless and invaluable especially the spiritual gifts, the physical and the intellectual or mental gifts proverbs 2:6 "For the Lord gives wisdom: out of his mouth cometh knowledge and understanding".

I see two basic motivating forces and they are love and gift. When you do these two, you spread joy to lives and when you love, you open to all that life has to offer with passion, excitement, and acceptance. You need to learn to love yourselves first, in all your glory and your imperfections. If you cannot love yourselves, you cannot fully open to your ability to love others or your potential to create.

Hear this, growth and all hopes for a better globe rest in the love and open-hearted vision of citizens who embrace love and gift. Remember the saying. "Givers never lack". While we were kids mum taught us how to give gifts. She always told us to always give gifts and be kind to people, in fact she made us practice giving things away on our own, not just things we don't really care about, things we really like. At first, the teaching wasn't making any sense to us until later we begin to feel good seeing others people using what we gave them. The size of the gift may not really matter, but what matters is the quality and the amount of mental attachment you overcome. That does not mean that you have to bankrupt yourself to give gifts, but it means that you should give good and quality gifts cheerfully.

"Money never made a man happy yet, nor will it.
The more a man has, the more he wants.
Instead of filling a vacuum, it makes one.

—Benjamin Franklin

On daily basics people spend money to obtain one thing or the other. Most people seem to have a morbid fascination with the way and means of spending money, spending money does not require advanced knowledge of the financial world, but discipline and good understanding of your need. It is important to differentiate what you need from what you want. When you study your income and budget, it will help you not to spend or use money carelessly. You must be self-discipline. Your money is not meant to buy anything or everything your eyes sees. You need to control your spending habit; failure to do that might lead you to debt and even course you trouble. Spending wisely goes beyond just money. In every aspect of life it is advisable that you conduct his yourself wisely. You may ask, How do I spend my money because I like to buy this and that?, safe the trouble and focus only on your basic needs, keep away from unnecessary thing, which you may not even use in the nearest future. First of all ask yourself, "Do I really need this?" If yes buy it, but if the no, then do not. Don't be too fast to get the latest fashion.

Living up with the latest trend, fad or fashion will effectively get you into debt, especially if you are not able to pay the bills. Be content with your present cell phone, don't plan on getting the latest brand, unless you can really afford it and you need it. 70% of those using smart phones today can't and don't even use half of its functions. Spending wisely will help you save your money. Everyone can spend money, but many do not truly spend it wisely. More importantly invest in yourself. Read books, explore, research, train, expand your skills, and learn another language or another sport. Several researches have proven that the pleasure of buying material things is immediate, but short lived. After a few days, you forget and take it for granted. Yesterday I stumble on the book of Isaiah 55:2 it says "why do you spend for what is not bread, and your wages for what does not satisfy" Therefore friends, whatever you do, however you do it, think before you act.

With all the money my uncle embezzled over the years, it's no surprise he lives in a gated community. But what is amazing, however, is that he somehow managed to get his own cell."

—Jarod Kintz

A mega businessman just added to his flicks of cars the latest customized 2013 Ferrari, it was a magnificent moving machine with the latest technology attached to it. You know, sometimes there are cars that makes you stop and shout wow!!! A kind of astonishment that suspends one's lips until the car fades away. Yea it's true, sometimes you can't just help it. This business mogul who is also the CEO of different conglomerates has special drivers, but this time he decided to drive his latest Ferrari and enjoy the sweet evening drive alone. As he was moving slowly enjoying his ride, suddenly an on-coming vehicle ran into his car and his Ferrari somersaulted and later came to rest. Fortunately, both occupants of the cars were alive, although injuries were sustained. The businessman jumped out with the little strength in him and with full anger, he reached to the man who hit his car trying to hit him with his right hand, but he was stopped by the crowd who rushed to the scene immediately. He began to shout and describing his beautiful car and how the man had damaged it. Then the police arrived at the horrible scene, and called for an ambulance while the man was still shouting for his car. The police man trying to calm the businessman down said "sir you are shouting at this man but your left hand is missing" . . . the businessman now looked at his hand and angrily shouted at the top of his voice, "where is my Rolex gold watch?". MAN AND MATERIAL THINGS. What is it that you have that matter so much that you can't let go? Some value money and value their partners; some can even kill to be in positions and authority. Remember Psalms 24:1-2 "the earth is the Lord's and the fullness therein, for He has founded it upon the seas, and established it upon the floods". While I leave you with these words from an anonymous writer, who having gleaned on this generation stated that. "Many years from now, it will not matter what kind of car you drove, what kind of house you live in. How much you had in your bank account or what your clothes looked like, but the world may be a little better because you were important in the life of a child"

To know what you prefer instead of humbly saying Amen to what the world tells you you ought to prefer, is to have kept your soul alive.

—Robert Louis Stevenson

It is true that achiever do not sit down and wait for success to come to them, they press on for success. A man who is determine to win must persevere till the end knowing that every good idea he develops has its own challenges, as such one must face every challenge with the aim of overcoming it. While searching for the pathway to Asia, Columbus was faced with incredible difficulties as he sails, he experienced different kinds of storms, hunger and discouragement in fact he was even face with losing his life. The crews of his three ships were near mutiny, but day-in-day-out he sailed on and his perseverance paid off as he found a new continents. Perseverance is needed to win the race. Strength of mind can turn complexity to simplicity, with perseverance Walt Disney's request for loan which was rejected by three hundred and one banks before he finally got approval, but because he refused to quit, in Florida he built the world most famous theme park.

Frank Tyger is an author who observes that in every triumph, there is a lot of try. Perseverance may mean more than just trying, it is an investment of some sort, it is a willingness to bind you emotionally, spiritually and physically to an idea, purpose or task until it has been completed. It is doing a lot more.

For you to build up yourself to persevere you must have a clear vision, everything that is great is actually created twice. First it is created mentally in your spirit and secondly it is created physically. Our creative ability comes from God who made us in His likeness (Genesis 1:27) a God given vision will keep you moving forward. Another thing is purpose; it is difficult to develop persistence when you lack a sense of purpose, and conversely, when you have a passionate sense of purpose, energy rises. Now think with me, what is that good thing that you have been planning to do. You know clearly in your spirit how you want it, but the will to start up is faint. This is the time to start up. Grip this opportunity and tell yourself you can do it by starting now.

It's the repetition of affirmations that leads to belief. And once that belief becomes a deep conviction, things begin to happen.

—Claude M. Bristol

The word affirmation is a statement of positive fact, a declaration that is true. Affirmation is at all times a word in the present and as a rule it starts with "I." Affirmations are intended to solidify what you believe about you. People who know the importance of affirmation never declare any bad word against their lives, they remain positive to every good thing they want and they affirm it. What you affirm now may be true in the future, but you must believe with all your heart and claim what you believe for your affirmation to materialize. Affirmations can be said anytime, anywhere, either silent or loud, but I prefer to say it loud so that the walls will hear. It is true that the more you affirm a thing with great believe, the more real, accurate, solid and firm they become.

Affirmations are very powerful. Try practicing it by repeating your affirmation in front of a mirror while looking into your eyes. As you do this, all the negative thoughts and feeling that keeps you from fulfilling your affirmation will show up. As they show up, don't stop; continue your affirmation and they will float away. In all your limitations a part of you knows the truth of the affirmation. It is important to set aside special time for affirmation, (I choose to do it during or after my morning prayer) sit in the sacred room, and say some special declaration again, again and again. You can also go to the mirror and watch yourself saying it and meaning it, then go out and live that declaration fully. How do I mean live it fully? You act in line with your affirmation by going your way and putting on "I can, I will" for that affirmation. Begin to practice everything you want and live the affirmation.

Above all, it is important to create affirmation that suits your exact circumstances and you must remember to keep them positively in the present. When making affirmation, you must be sure about what you say. Remember, there is a different between "I am great, I am wealthy and I am the best" from "I want to be great, I want to be wealthy and I want to be the best" or "very soon, if am lucky, I'll be great, I'll be wealthy and I'll be the best". Read what Norman Vincent Peale said about affirmation, he said "Watch your manner of speech if you wish to develop a peaceful state of mind. Start each day by affirming peaceful, contented and happy attitudes and your days will tend to be pleasant and successful."

I think self-awareness is probably the most important thing towards being a champion.

—Billie Jean King

By now, I know you know who you are, what you want, what you need, where you want to go, what you want to do and all of that, but knowing this and all of that is not enough until you start working towards achieving what you know. If you truly want to get where you want to be, then you have to work hard to get there as a champion. As you know, there are different kinds of people when it comes to winning; the potential champions, this is described as those who are yet to be champions, in other words they are working hard to be champions someday. Current champions, these are people who are existing in their greatness and presently they are reigning as champions, and finally the ex-champions. These are those who were once champions, they reined greatly, but suddenly they fall off. As such, they no longer occupy the position as current champions, they become ex-champions.

Now it is important to know that virtually everyone belongs to the first category, some get to the second category and remain there while many still falls to the third category. Everyone was born into this world with the potential of becoming a champion. Everyone has a gift of greatness in them, but as you would expect, it is one thing to have the potential to be great, and it is in every respect a different ball game to run with the dream and actualize greatness. Just like every man is a prospective father, but not all men become fathers. The same applies to women who had the potential of becoming a mother and eventually became one. Everyone wants to be rich, but everyone is not rich. The dream to be the best in your career is a prospect or a viewpoint, that is the potential you posses for your career. Actualizing your dream and living in your dream makes you an existing champion. This is when you dream of being the best in your career and you are actually the best, at this point you are an existing or current champion. Now, most people don't just dream, they actually actualize their dreams, but along the line they miss out. That is why they are regarded as ex-champions. You will agree with me, nobody celebrates you just because you have a dream; you are celebrated when you actualize your dream. Therefore, push on to be current champion by tracking every of your potential logically to be and remain the current champion.

I once knew a king, who does not know the king in him, I also knew a man who operates like a king, but we are born kings, we operate and takes order from the king of kings that is always with us

Finally, permit me to draw your attention to Rodeo sport. It is one of the most dangerous sports especially with bull riding, it involves a rider seating on a colossal bull and trying to hang on even as the bull attempts to buck off or throw off the rider. Universally, it is a truth acknowledged that this sport is an interesting game to watch. However, it is a dangerous sport for the participants, even though they knew for sure that they could be hurt someday, they still love to play the game. In fact there is a popular saying that "it's not if you get hurt, it's when." That is to say, riders are certain to be hurt someday. Well, you may not easily get a perfect bull rider because rodeo sport requires moral fiber, flexibility, sense of equilibrium, skill and boldness.

Prince William (Duke of Cambridge) is the elder son of Diana, Princess of Wales, and Charles, Prince of Wales; he is third-eldest grandchild of Queen Elizabeth II and Prince Philip, Duke of Edinburgh, Prince William really like rodeo sport. In fact sometimes he takes his wife Kate to watch the game. Sometimes last month he was out for his usually rodeo sports, he nodded his head to let go the bull through the gate. As soon as the bull was let out of the fence, he was seated on the bull with one of his hands on the rope riding and trying to gain balance as he enjoys his ride. But then the bull was becoming aggressive, jumping up and down wagging her tale and shaking her body to buck off the rider. This was done severally until Prince William lost balance and fail off. The bull ran off and turns back with fierceness to fight the rider. Naturally every bull rider would run for a defense because the bull at that point can kill the rider, but prince William did not run, rather he stood firm. Just some seconds before the bull could hit him, the guards shot the bull.

When asked "why didn't you run for your life" in fact I lover his response he said kings don't run. He added that he would rather die as a king than run for a bull" his answer teaches a lot if you can reflect on the king in you. How often have you been running away from mere challenges? For prince Williams he knew that his guards would not allow him to be killed by a bull, even if they do, he would rather die as a king than to run for a bull. Reflect on this, who are you and what do you run for? Think of it, if the king of kings is your father why are you running away from mere challenges?